21 WAYS TO BRING BALANCE INTO YOUR LIFE

RHONA PARSONS
The Balance Coach

Awareness is the beginning of change

RUBY BLUE PUBLISHING

Published by Ruby Blue Publishing.

For information visit: www.rhonaparsons.com

Cover design by Shine Creative: www.shine-creative.ca

ISBN: 978-1-7753293-0-5

First edition: September 2018

Dear Human:

You've got it all wrong. You didn't come here
to master unconditional love. That is where
you came from and where you'll return.
You came here to learn personal love.
Universal love. Messy love. Sweaty love.
Crazy love. Broken love. Whole love.
Infused with divinity. Loved through the
grace of stumbling. Demonstrated
through the beauty of…messing up.
Often. You didn't come here to be perfect.
You already are. You came here to be
gorgeously human. Flawed and fabulous.
And then to rise again into remembering.
But unconditional love? Stop telling that story.
Love, in truth, doesn't need ANY other adjectives. It doesn't
require modifiers. It doesn't require the condition of perfection.
It only asks that you show up. And do your best. That you
stay present and feel fully. That you shine and fly and laugh
and cry and hurt and heal and fall and get back up and play
and work and live and die as YOU. It's enough. It's plenty."

Courtenay A Walsh

Table of Contents

INTRODUCTION

Bringing Balance to your Body, Mind, and Spirit

YOU CAN CREATE AND LIVE
A HEALTHY, FUN-FILLED LIFE!

Creating and living a healthy fun-filled lifestyle takes time, energy, and an investment in your #1 asset – YOU!

We are here to experience life. Our experience is driven by our thoughts and emotions which come from only two sources — fear or love. We have only three choices in this lifetime: to give in, give up or live our life to the fullest, giving it all we've got!

Our body is the most amazing machine in the world, yet so many of us don't think about our health until we are sick or broken. As sad as it sounds, some people look after their vehicles better than their bodies. Without good health and proper maintenance, happiness will elude us. It doesn't matter how much money we have, how many toys we own or how many beautiful dresses we have hanging in our closet; without our health, we can't enjoy any of it. All our other first world problems no longer matter when being sick becomes our #1 problem. I believe we can all live healthier lives by following certain principles that will allow us to enjoy every day and live life to the fullest.

Why does it matter?
Principles guide us, they define us and help us to live centered fulfilling lives.

If you fail to plan, you plan to fail. It's that simple. The 21 methods in this book will help you create the balanced life that you've always dreamed of having. This guide can be used by scanning through the pages and seeing where your thoughts take you **OR** you can start at the beginning. My suggestion to you is to choose one tip that resonates with you, one that you are not already doing in your life and commit to mastering it before beginning another.

I've always been proud of the fact that I'm a multi-tasker, but my way of thinking is changing. When I'm feeling overwhelmed, I am more effective at tackling my 'to do' list one task at a time. I prioritize and deal with each task individually. Trying this approach can help establish new discipline in your life, bringing with it all that your heart desires.

How do you do it?
Before you can start changing your life to create balance, you need to do a quick check on where you are in each area. Look at the pie chart on the next page. Each piece of the pie represents one part of your life. Using a scale of 1-10, you are

going to decide how each part of your life scores; a score of one is low on the contentment scale, and ten means that you are good to go!

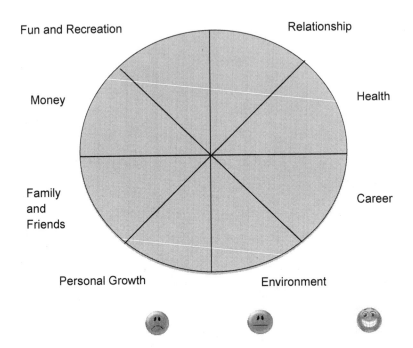

Fun and Recreation 1 2 3 4 5 6 7 8 9 10
Are you having fun? Taking time to do the things you love to do?

Money   **1 2 3 4 5 6 7 8 9 10**
Money is important as we need it to live and survive; are you struggling?

Family and Friends 1 2 3 4 5 6 7 8 9 10
Our loved ones are the reason to live and make a living; are you happy?

Personal Growth   **1 2 3 4 5 6 7 8 9 10**
Are you working towards personal goals? Are you where you want to be?

Relationship   **1 2 3 4 5 6 7 8 9 10**
For some of us it's important to have a companion; for others not...
you may be very content being single

Health   **1 2 3 4 5 6 7 8 9 10**
Without which nothing makes sense; how is your health?

Career   **1 2 3 4 5 6 7 8 9 10**
Are you passionate about your work? Love what you're doing?

Environment   **1 2 3 4 5 6 7 8 9 10**
Do positive people surround you? Nature? Fresh air? Family?

Once you've scored each area of your life, place each number onto the pie chart (1 is the centre of the pie and 10 on the outer edge) and join the dots. Have you drawn a perfect circle? Is the circle a little off balance? If any area of your life is off a little, your chart will be out of balance. It's tough to work on all eight aspects of your life at once. Quite often, as we begin to put the pieces together, everything else falls into place. Which aspect of your life do you believe needs the most attention? Write it here:

_____

"Awareness is the beginning of change" - Rhona

Now that you've chosen the area of your life that you want to bring balance to, here are a few ideas that will help to plan the rest of your life:

1. **According to Buddha, "When the student is ready, the teacher will appear".** Become an observer of your thoughts and actions. Notice all the synchronicities that may be conspiring to help you achieve your potential.

4

2. **Feel gratitude for all the things that are happening in your life.** Before I go to sleep every night, I think about and feel in my heart three things that I am grateful for that have made me happy during the day. Be thankful for those things that make you happy.

3. **Live an authentic and meaningful life.** Be true to yourself and live in line with your values. Ask yourself, "What do I want in my life? What small steps can I take to move in the direction of living my life to the fullest?" And then do it.

4. **Take each day as it comes.** What is the saying? "Yesterday was the past; tomorrow is the future, today is the present – enjoy the gift." Begin each day with a new slate; smile, feel the love in your heart and go out and enjoy every moment of your day.

5. **Look after your body.** Enjoy every meal, snack, chocolate, cheese, wine or beer but always remember the 80:20 rule (more information on page 20). Dance like no-one's watching, exercise, ski, swim, go for a walk or ride your bike...just keep moving!

6. **Try not to change everything at once.** Create significant changes by taking baby steps. You will notice that some ideas are repeated often in the

upcoming chapters. Repetition is the key to bringing about positive change, and the more we repeat ideas and goals, the quicker we will reap the rewards.

"Sometimes the smallest step in the right direction ends up being the biggest step of your life. Tiptoe if you must but take the step."
Naeem Callaway

BREATHE

What is it?

Breath is fundamental to life. We take our first breath at birth and our last when we leave this beautiful place. Breathing is the most unconscious thing that we do and is controlled by our central nervous system from birth to death. When we breathe normally, there is so much going on in our body, that unless we consciously focus on each movement, some of us are oblivious to the wonders of the breath.

According to an article written in the Herald Tribune in 2010, an average person **at rest** takes about **16 breaths** per minute, about **960 breaths** an hour, **23,040 breaths** a day, and **8,409,600** a year. Can you imagine how many breaths a person takes when being active? A person who lives to 80 will take approximately **672,768,000 breaths** in a lifetime; that is a lot of breathing!

Why does it matter?

Most of us live in a society of stress and move at a fast pace which unconsciously may be causing us to breathe very shallow into our chest and shoulders, and only using the upper third of our lungs. Over time, if we live in a stressed state, this shallow breathing pattern becomes our normal pattern.

This shallow breathing can put the body into a stressed state, a fight/flight response, because it believes that it is getting attacked from an outside source. When this happens, many things begin to co-occur in our body but specifically, two hormones get released into our bloodstream: **Adrenaline** and **Cortisol**. Adrenaline increases the heart rate, raises blood pressure and boosts energy supplies. Cortisol increases glucose (sugar) into the bloodstream. Lots of other things are happening at the same time, and the body is set to flee from danger. The problem is that nowadays we are not in a 'life or death' situation every day; we are simply stressed out from life! When our body releases too much Cortisol, it can end up sitting in our belly fat, increasing our muffin top by inches, and stressing us out even more.

I experienced 'Cortisol belly' first hand 11 years ago. My hubby became very sick in 2006, and I was working full-time as a manager of a group fitness department. I loved my position, working every day with a fantastic group of women. I taught 15 classes a week and was working full time at home too without help from anyone. Life was stressful, and I was getting a belly, and I couldn't understand what was going on. I wasn't overeating; I was exercising daily and thought I had a handle on life. It was because emotionally I was stressed to the max. Despite my active lifestyle, my body was producing too much Cortisol, and my belly was growing. I realized that my body was in constant fight/flight mode, so I researched Cortisol and its effects from stress. I had many symptoms. I began practicing different ways of breathing and concluded that a person could not be stressed out and breathe deeply at the same time. It's not the way the body works.

One more critical piece of information for us ladies:
Many women, of all ages, suffer from urinary incontinence when they jump, sneeze, laugh, run or any other activity that makes them pee in their pants. Most women believe this is caused by having children and/or getting older. Guess what? One of the reasons is because the pelvic floor has been weakened by having children. It's a fitness problem with a fitness solution, and part of that solution is to learn how to breathe correctly.

If you watch a sleeping baby breathe, the breathing is very slow and rhythmic. When a baby breathes in, the clavicle (collarbone) lifts, the rib muscles expand the ribs, and the belly rises. When the baby breathes out, the clavicle lowers, the rib muscles (between the ribs) contract and the belly falls; this is a fully relaxed breath, a complete breath. I had to learn how to breathe naturally. Mastering the "**Complete Breath Technique**" helped me to start bringing relaxation into my life.

How do you do it?

This drawing shows the diaphragm. It is dome-shaped and divides the chest from the abdomen and is the primary muscle for *breathing. **The diaphragm and pelvic floor move together with the breath. (Think of the pelvic floor as dome-shaped too).**

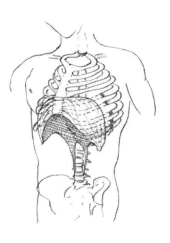

Each time we take a breath in, our clavicle lifts, the rib muscles expand, the diaphragm contracts (the dome flattens down), the belly pushes outward, and the pelvic floor flattens down moving away from the body. When we breathe out, the reverse happens. The pelvic floor 'domes' up, the belly lowers toward the spine pushing the diaphragm back up, the breath is pushed out of the lungs by the rib muscles contracting, the clavicle lowers, and the air is then forced out through the mouth or nose.

*Other muscles play roles in breathing as well, but we are just focusing on the primary ones.

PRACTICE TIP

Slowly read the following exercise into a recording device, (your phone or voice recorder) and then play it each time you do the breathing exercise. An audio recording will allow you to relax and focus on the **Complete Breath Technique** instead of stopping and starting to read each step.

How to master the Complete Breath Technique:

1. Lie down on the floor with both hands on your belly, fingertips touching.

2. Close your eyes, slowly breathe in (inhale) through your nose and visualize the diaphragm flattening down, gently pushing your belly out (fingertips will come apart). Breathe out (exhale) and feel the belly dropping toward the spine (fingers will go back together) and visualize the diaphragm floating back up (doming). Continue this for a few breaths and feel the belly rising and falling.

3. Now place one hand on your rib cage and one hand on your clavicle; inhale and feel the ribs expand and clavicle rise into your hands; notice the belly rising. Exhale and feel the belly dropping, the ribs gently contracting (coming in) and the clavicle lowering.

11

Continue this for a few breaths, still visualizing the diaphragm flattening and 'doming,'

4. Continue breathing this way, inhaling and feeling the ribs expand; the clavicle and belly rise and the pelvic floor flatten. Exhale, pelvic floor domes, belly drops, ribs come in, and the clavicle drops. Continue for 2 - 4 breaths.

5. Stay here for a few minutes relaxing and mastering the **Complete Breath Technique**. Allow your body to melt into the floor, thoroughly relaxing. Stay in this position for as long as you like.

Urinary incontinence can be improved by mastering the breath. Begin to actively contract the pelvic floor muscles as you exhale and release it when you inhale.

By practicing and mastering the **Complete Breath Technique**, you will reap many rewards. There are too many rewards to list here, but these three are very important to know:

- Your nervous system will start to relax, bringing relaxation to your body
- Your resting heart rate will slow down, meaning that it won't have to work so hard all the time
- Your immune system will become stronger, and you will become a healthier, happier you!

SLEEP

What is it?

Along with nutrition and exercise, sleep is a hugely important part of our life. Do you know that we spend roughly a third of our lives sleeping? When we are asleep the nervous system is somewhat inactive; the eyes are closed, the body is relaxed, and our consciousness is suspended. We get regenerated when we sleep.

Why does it matter?

If we don't get quality sleep every night, we suffer the next day. We can feel tired and irritable, we don't function as well, and we can make mistakes.

The general rule of thumb, from my research, is that the average adult should get at least 8 hours sleep every night, but most of us sleep between 6 - 7 ½ hours. Some people sleep a lot longer and some only need 6 hours. Which one are you?

I sleep, on an average, 7½ hours a night. Most nights I sleep all night (depending if hubby's working nights because then I get the whole bed to myself ☺), but there are those nights when I wake up 2-3 times, and it can get pretty frustrating. It can be because our kitty, Ruby, decides she's going to take up all of my leg room. It can be because I drank wine late in the evening (and our liver detoxes around 3 am every night) or that I drank too much water too close to bedtime.

If you aren't sleeping well, why do you think it is?

_____

_____

_____

Getting a good night's sleep can be disrupted by stress in our life. Let's think about this for a minute. When we're stressed, we usually have a hard time sleeping because our mind won't shut off from all the worry, doubt or fears that we may be feeling. Is there any stress in your life? Are you experiencing daily any of the following? (Mark an X to all that apply)

Frustrated and/or angry ____

High blood pressure ____

Heart palpitations ____

Irritated most of the time ____

Have a continuous headache ____

Not eating well; loss of appetite ____

Have an upset stomach; gut ache ____

Shoulders and neck are stiff ____

Sad; feelings of despair   ——

Diarrhea/constipation   ——

Rashes and hives   ——

Insomnia   ——

How do you do it?

Awareness is the beginning of change.

You may not even be aware that something is bothering you and it's stopping you from having a good night's sleep and enjoying life to the fullest. If you are experiencing any of the symptoms in the previous list, use this space to write down why you're feeling this way. What is making your body act this way?

_____

_____

_____

The next questions to ask yourself:

1. "Is there anything I can do to get rid of this stress?"

_____

2. "What will make me feel better?"

_____

3. "Do I have any control over the outcome?"

_____

One thing I learned a long time ago was that I carried a lot of other people's stresses, and when I learned that what happened to others was none of my business, my life became a whole lot lighter. We must remember that everyone here is on their journey, even our children. Sure, we are responsible for our children, and we help them as much as we can; the answer is to take action and break the cycle of worry and stress. It's about living in the present moment (there's more information in Chapter 11). Do I worry about the future? Nope! Do I plan for the future? Yes I do, but I live each day to the fullest and don't worry about tomorrow. As I always say, I could get hit and killed by a runaway vehicle tomorrow so why worry about something that may never happen!

A few years ago a study was completed about worry. According to Don Joseph Goewey, author of *The End of Stress, 4 Steps to Rewire Your Brain,* the study showed that 85% of things that individuals worried about never happened. With the 15% that did happen, 79% of the people realized that it wasn't as bad as they thought it would be! 97% of what we worry about is no more than our mind (ego) creating illusions of embellishment and confusion.

What can you do to get a good night's sleep EVERY night?
As with all things, I believe that firstly, you need a routine. Secondly, make your bed upon waking (a made bed always looks so much more inviting to me) and thirdly, reserve your bed and bedroom for sleeping, making love and relaxing. No books, computers, phones or televisions should be in the

bedroom as they can train the brain to stay awake. Falling asleep with the TV on doesn't allow your body and mind to go into deep sleep mode, making you feel exhausted upon waking the next morning. Here are some suggestions for you to create a great bedtime routine:

1. Get ready for bed at the same time every night.

2. Turn off the TV about a ½ hour before bedtime and get ready for bed.

3. Take a few minutes to relax and stretch. (Any quiet, undisturbed place will do) and practice the **Complete Breath Technique** (page 11).

4. Drink your favourite chamomile tea.

5. Make sure your bedroom is cold and dark. (I make sure I am warm enough in bed by adding an extra blanket if it's a cold night).

6. Set your alarm for the morning and leave your phone/clock in another room, so you're not disturbed by someone calling or the ticking of the clock.

7. Once in bed, think of 3 things you are grateful for that happened during your day; things that put a smile on your face and a pleasant feeling in your heart.

8. Practice the **Complete Breath Technique** again, and, when thoroughly relaxed.

9. Move into your favourite sleep position, close your eyes and ultimately let go; tomorrow is a new day. 💜

Do you already have a routine that you do every night? Write it here, and if you don't, this is the perfect time to create one:

_____

_____

_____

_____

_____

NUTRITION

What is it?

Simply said, nutrition is the study of the nutrients in food at work in our bodies; one source of energy that keeps us alive. Proper nutrition is about eating a healthy and balanced diet. Have you heard the phrase "You are what you eat"?

Why does it matter?

Food and drink provide the energy and nutrients you need to be healthy. Understanding what you eat, and drink is important because what you ingest on a day-to-day basis has an enormous impact on how your body functions and feels.

How do you do it?

I could write a whole book on nutrition, but I'm not going to as there are so many out there, and I'm not a Nutritionist. Instead, I'm going to share with you what has worked for me for the last 20 years of my life.

I believe that food is one of life's pleasures, but we must be smart about it. We need to balance our food intake with some form of exercise to burn off those extra calories that we are eating.

When working privately with clients, I get them to complete a 3-day eating journal so that we can figure out what they are eating every day. I found that those who wanted to lose weight were consuming on average 40% fewer calories than their BMR (basic metabolic rate – calories that the body needs to survive when we are at rest). **Eating less than our BMR can put us into starvation mode** (the body begins to reserve all foods coming in).

I believe in the 80:20 rule, which is more about eating healthy than being on a diet. I eat very healthy 80% of the time and indulge in my favourite foods 20% of the time. I always eat a combination of **MACRO NUTRIENTS** at each meal: *protein (chicken, fish, some beef, pork, a little tofu, shellfish, etc.), **complex carbohydrates (veggies, beans, whole grains) and

---

MACRO NUTRIENTS

*Protein is essential for building and maintaining your muscles and organs.

**Carbohydrates (CHO) are the primary source of energy for the body.

***Fats are essential for good health.

***fats. I still drink wine and I love eating cheese, crackers, and chocolate too.

The calories you ingest should always equal or be less than the calories you use (exercise). I can't eat by the 80:20 rule and not exercise. I would become very unhealthy and not feel good at all. Nutrition and exercise; the two go hand in hand.

Here's a great example of one of my 20% treats. Every six months or so I go to one of the local drive-thru restaurants and order one of my favourite meals; french fries, onion rings, and a hamburger — I love it! I call this my "6-month cleanse" (insert hearty laugh). You see, because I only eat this meal every six months or so, my body doesn't recognize it as the food I usually eat, so it gets eliminated (the natural way) the very next morning. Now, if I were to begin eating this more regularly, it would start 'sticking' to my body, and that is not a good thing!

When I first became a Personal Trainer, I read a lot about many different eating programs and diets and I tried a few. Some programs were too much work, most cut out my favourite foods, and some didn't work at all. For example, I stayed on the grape diet for only three days because you can only eat so many grapes!

What did, and still does, work for me was to learn how to read a nutritional label and always keep track of what I was eating and drinking. I did this for about three weeks the first time. I'm

21

a very habitual person when it comes to eating so even now, 21 years later, I know what I'm putting in my mouth and can keep everything under control. However, this takes time and practice. Eating small, well-balanced meals throughout the day, with plenty of fresh fruit and vegetables, keeps my energy up and minimizes mood swings. (You don't want to see me when I run out of energy; I get HANGRY!)

Do you know how to read a nutritional label?

Here are the first things you should know:

1-gram carbohydrate = 4 calories
1-gram protein   = 4 calories
1-gram fat   = 9 calories
1-gram sugar   = 4.5 teaspoons

Sodium intake should not exceed 2000 mg/day

Here is a typical nutritional label. The calories are for one serving (1 cup).

Total calories: *250
Fat   12g x 9 = 108 calories
CHO   31g x 4 = 124 calories
Protein 5g x 4 = 20 calories
Sugars = 5g
Sodium 210 mg
*The totals of the macro nutrients don't always add up to the total calories shown.

Nutrition Facts

Servings Per Container 2
Serving Size 1 cup (228g)

Amount Per Serving

Calories 250

	% Daily Value*
Total Fat 12g	18%
Saturated Fat 3g	15%
Trans Fat 3g	
Cholesterol 30mg	10%
Sodium 470mg	20%
Total Carbohydrate 31g	10%
Dietary Fiber 0g	0%
Sugars 5g	
Protein 5g	

In summary, this one food is approximately 43% fat, 49% carbohydrates (CHO), and only 8% protein. You can see why it is helpful to write out your food intake for a few days to see what the total food is that you eat daily.

I use the following daily percentages to manage my diet: 20% fat, 30% protein, and 50% carbohydrates. This formula keeps my weight in check and me on track. Sometimes when life gets in the way or gets too good (think Mexico), I get back on track by writing my foods down for three days.

So how do you know how many calories you should be eating? The Basic Metabolic Rate formula uses the totals of your height, weight, age and gender and calculates your BMR. You then use the **Harris Benedict Equation** that uses your BMR and applies an activity factor to calculate your daily needs.

Go to the following website to calculate your BMR and activity level:
http://www.bmi-calculator.net/bmr-calculator/

BMR: _____ + Activity Level: _____

= _____Calories needed daily.

My daily BMR is 1301.95 calories; this is just for me to be at rest. To find out my daily calorie needs, I multiply my activity level (moderately active) 1.55 by 1301.95 (my BMR) which totals 2020 calories. This total is the number of calories I should ingest daily to maintain my weight.

The journal below is my food diary from a typical day:

C= Cup	TOTAL CALORIES	FAT (g)	CHO (g)	PROTEIN (g)	Sodium (mg) < 2000 mg per day	Sugars (g) Approx. 25g per day
BREAKFAST: ¾C frozen blueberries	80	0	19	1	10	13
2C fresh spinach	20	0	3	2	80	0
One scoop Protein powder (Isagenix) Coffee	118.5	2.5	12	12	85	5.5
SNACK: 3 tbsp. hummus	90	6	6	3	65	0
Beet crackers (16 crackers) Coffee	135	7	16	2	50	1
LUNCH: Multi-grain bun	205	5	34	6	410	2
½ tbsp. mayonnaise	20	2	.5	0	40	0
½C roast chicken	176	4	0	35	84	0
½ C fresh spinach	5	0	.7	.5	20	0
½ tomato	16		3	1	4	2
1oz cheddar cheese	109	9	0	7	230	0
SNACK: Four dried prunes	100	0	24	1	0	15
DINNER: ½ lb teriyaki salmon	230	6	10	34	0	3
¾C white sushi rice	177	1	39	3	5	0
spinach salad	48	0	9	3		
One piece of dark chocolate	59	4	5	.75	9	4.5
TOTALS:	1588.5 cals	46.5g	181.2g	111.25g		
	x9	x4	x4			
	418.5g	**724.8**	**445g**			
Total percentage of calories	1588.5 26%	1588.5 46%	1588.5 28%		1092mg	46g

24

Looking at the information in my journal, I see that my caloric intake is lower than the daily 2020 calories that I should be ingesting, but I'm not concerned about that as I do make sure that I eat more than my BMR every day. The numbers show that my sugar intake is higher than it should be, but the majority came from fruit, which are natural sugars. My fat intake is a little higher than I like it to be but most of it was good fat. I'm habitual every day with my breakfast and snacks, and I will sometimes have a glass of wine with dinner too…but again, it's all about balance. My activities yesterday were teaching 2 Pilates classes and going for a 25-minute walk last evening. I also drink 8 cups of water daily as well. (see Chapter 4 for Drinking Water)

Figuring out your daily caloric intake by writing down everything you eat may not be for you, but I can guarantee that once you realize what you are putting in your body, you will change the way you look at food.

Portion control is a significant attribute to eating healthy and wisely. The Canada Food Guide has some great information on serving sizes. You can easily find information on the internet or at your local Nutritionist's office.

If you're the least bit curious about your eating habits, use the blank food diary sheet on page 27. Print three copies and keep track for three days (I recommend doing it for at least a week if you need to get a handle on your food). Don't change your eating habits; you want your diary to represent what you eat daily.

I'm sure you will agree that you want to have more energy, feel great and be able to always wear the clothes in your closet. When you can figure out the right amount of food to eat, and the right foods to eat, your body will start changing for the better.

Don't worry about what the scale says; your clothes will let you know when you've gained weight! If you would like to download the food diary sheet on a full-sized page, go to www.rhonaparsons.com/21ways

	TOTAL CALORIES	FAT (g)	CHO (g)	PROTEIN (g)	Sodium (mg) < 2000 mg per day	Sugars (g) Approx. 25g per day
BREAKFAST:						
SNACK:						
LUNCH:						
SNACK:						
DINNER:						
TOTALS: Total of calories		x9	x4	x4		
Divided by total grams = percentage						

Notes

DRINK WATER

What is it?

We humans can go weeks without eating but only a few days without water; we need to drink water to survive. Do you know that your body is made up of approximately 60% water? Our brain is 70% water and our lungs, nearly 90%!

Why does it matter?

Jen Laskey, a New York City-based Freelance Writer, Editor, and Digital Media Strategist, wrote and explained that our body uses water to help regulate temperature and to maintain bodily functions. Because we lose water through breathing, sweating, urination, and digestion, it's important to rehydrate by drinking fluids and eating foods that contain water every day.

Water does more than quench your thirst and regulate your body's temperature. It also keeps the tissues in your body moist. You know how it feels when your eyes, nose, or mouth gets dry? Keeping your body hydrated helps it retain optiMum levels of moisture in these sensitive areas, as well as in the blood, bones, and the brain. Also, water helps protect the spinal cord, and it acts as a lubricant and cushion for your joints. Each day, your body must replace approximately 2.5 liters of water through ingested liquid and foods.

Many mineral nutrients are essential for maintaining fluid balance in the body. A few that come to my mind are potassium, calcium, phosphorus, and magnesium. You can easily find information on all four of these minerals on the internet or at your local Nutritionist's office.

The most familiar one to us all is plain old table salt – Sodium. Why is this important? Sodium helps your body absorb and retain more water.

> **Analogy: Think about the motor oil you use in your car; it doesn't make the engine run, but it is necessary to keep everything running smoothly!**

To function normally, most adults require approximately 500mg sodium through diet daily, and athletes need up to 2000mg sodium. Unfortunately, from what I've read, most Canadians get too much sodium, and it's usually from our diet. Too much salt retains excess fluid in the body and can make you feel bloated.

How much water should you drink a day?

Most health authorities say we should drink at least 8 cups (2 litres) of water per day. **This amount is known as the 8x8 rule.** The question many ask is "can you drink too much water?" From what I've read, it is virtually impossible for a healthy person, on a healthy diet, to drink himself/herself to death on water.

With some illnesses, water intake should be kept to a minimum or under the guidance of your health professional. Examples of these are cardiovascular disease, high blood pressure, and heart failure.

Too much fluid in your body can make it harder for a weakened heart to pump. I learned a lot about sodium when my hubby was diagnosed with Congestive Heart Failure twelve years ago. We had to cut out a lot of sodium from our foods for him. Our food became very bland until we started adding more herbs to our meals and used a salt-less cocktail of herbs (think Mrs. Dash). It took about six weeks for our palates to get used to our new way of eating. Because of how active I was though, my legs would start to cramp when I was teaching aerobics, so I needed to add a little more salt into my diet.

How about not enough water? As I said earlier, the body is 60% water, so we need to drink a considerable amount daily. Thirst and dryness in your mouth is usually the first sign of dehydration; the second is reduced and dark coloured urine. Inconsistency in drinking water can cause the body to retain the fluid you have drank which will make you feel bloated and create weight gain!

Still not sure if drinking water is for you? Look at these benefits:

- Increases energy and relieves fatigue
- Promotes weight loss
- Flushes out toxins
- Improves skin complexion
- Maintains regularity
- Boosts immune system
- Relieves headaches
- Prevents muscles cramping

How do you do it?

How can you make drinking water become a habit for you?

I believe that consistency is essential; you must drink the same amount of water EVERY DAY and have it with you. When you first start, you'll feel like you're going to the bathroom all the time. It is possible that you will be, but it will only last for about three days. Once you are consistently drinking the same amount of water every day, your body will hit a point of equilibrium, and you'll get into a normal rhythm of going to the bathroom every 2-3 hours.

Here are two ways that have worked for me to become consistent in drinking water:

1. Water bottles come in many sizes, shapes, and colors; I use two bottles. I have an 8-cup (2 litre) water bottle (shown) that I fill every morning. This bottle keeps me on track of how much water I have drank during the day and how much I have to drink before I have my glass of wine in the evening. The other bottle I have holds 2 cups of  water, and I carry it with me all day and fill up from the 8-cup container.

33

2. If I am travelling and can't bring my 8-cupper with me, I will put four hair elastics around my 2-cup bottle. Every time I empty the bottle, I take one of the elastics off. It's a great way to keep track of what I've had to drink. It's so easy when I'm out of my routine to forget to drink my water.

Find a way that will help you get into the habit of drinking at least 8 cups of water a day. Your body will thank you.

EXERCISE

What is it?

As I said at the beginning of this book, the human body is the most amazing machine in the world! It is meant to move effortlessly with ease and grace, not sit behind a desk for hours at a time, behind the wheel of a car, or on a couch for hours watching television. It needs physical exercise. Your body needs to do some type of daily activity for your overall health and wellness.

Why does it matter?

If you have never been someone who exercised, hated gym class at school, and would rather sit and read a book or do some handwork, I need to tell you that it is crucial for you to start. Why do I say this? As a personal trainer, I have worked with many people who have never exercised and then either became injured, sick, or diagnosed with a disease that forced them to exercise. It wasn't fun for them, and it was tough for me to keep them motivated because they didn't want to be there.

One disease that mostly affects women is Osteoporosis. Simply put, Osteoporosis is a disease that is recognized by low bone mass and the deterioration of bone tissue. It's known as the "Silent Thief" according to www.osteoporosis.ca because bone deterioration can happen over some years without being detected until a person falls and breaks a bone.

More and more research support exercise as the number one antidote for avoiding certain diseases - it comes back to my first paragraph of this chapter - the body is meant to move.

There are so many other benefits for why you should exercise; do any of these speak to you?

- Improves your health
- Strengthens your muscles and your cardiovascular system
- Reduces your risk of heart disease
- Improves your quality of life; prevents aging
- Increases your energy; burns off unwanted calories
- Increases your feel-good hormones
- Relieves stress and depression
- Increases happiness
- Boosts your immunes system, confidence and self-esteem
- Helps prevent type-2 diabetes and obesity
- Increases quality of sleep

Physically, exercise releases the feel-good chemicals in our brain known as neurotransmitters and endorphins. For me, there is nothing better than getting out in nature to bring me to a great place emotionally. My endorphins kick in and return me to feelings of ease and contentment. Sometimes I have to kick my butt out the door, but I love going walking, and once I make up my mind, I put on my shoes and jacket, grab my walking poles and out the door I go. Going walking helps put life into perspective for me and helps to put my plans into action. I usually come home with great ideas. I've even been known to record my thoughts on my walks so that I don't forget them once I get back home.

How do you do it?

So how can you have fun keeping your body in great shape, stop gaining weight and relieve tension, create greater mobility, strength, and health? You need to move because when you do, you will receive immediate and long-term health benefits! The first thing you need to do is pick something that you love doing. What do you like to do regarding physical activity? Your pick is the first ingredient to success. If you begin something that you don't enjoy, you will only last a little while before you stop.

What did you do for activity as a child that you loved? This is always a great place to look back on. Write it here:

_____

I grew up in the south of England and loved going for walks through the countryside. In high school I was a short-distance track runner, played netball and I LOVED to dance!

One thing I detested was cross-country running…ugh! I used to begin the run with a couple of friends, and we would hide in the bushes and wait for the first few runners to go by and then join the group. It worked great until we got distracted one day and by the time we got back to the locker room, everyone was showered and dressed. We were in hot water with our teacher! You won't see me out running, and if you do, you better be able to run faster than me because something will be chasing me!

Do you have a favourite type of exercise? What do you love to do that makes you feel great, puts a smile on your face and gives you that feeling of contentment and joy? Write it here:

_____

Here are some examples of different ways to exercise. They are broken down into categories. The word 'weight-bearing' means when your body works against the forces of gravity and these are some of the best types of exercises to do. Pick all the exercises that interest you:

LOW IMPACT WEIGHT-BEARING EXERCISES
- Low Impact Aerobics (cardio – low intensity)
- Walking
- Treadmill walking
- Stationary bicycle riding
- Elliptical training
- Swimming

HIGH IMPACT WEIGHT-BEARING EXERCISES
- High Impact Aerobics (cardio – high intensity)
- Dancing
- Hiking
- Jogging
- Pickle ball
- Tennis
- Volleyball

- Basketball
- Cycling
- Ballet
- Jazz Dancing
- Boxing

MUSCLE STRENGTHENING EXERCISES

- Weight Lifting
- Using weight machines
- Suspension straps (bodyweight exercises)
- Latex resistance bands and exercise tubing

CORE, FLEXIBILITY AND BALANCE EXERCISES

- Pilates
- Yoga
- Core-specific classes
- Ballet

As you can see, there are so many things to do to keep your heart healthy, your bones strong, and to keep the spring in your step. You don't have to join a gym to lift weights or a dance class to dance if you don't like being in a group atmosphere. Personally, I am more motivated when I get to work out alongside women and men who are there for the same reason I am; to stay healthy and active and to live life to the fullest! What is first on your agenda?

S-T-R-E-T-C-H

There were two things I wanted to accomplish growing up; to touch my toes and to whistle. When I went to my first Yoga class at the age of 36, I didn't realize how tight my body was, and it was in that class that I decided I was going to do everything I could to touch my toes! I'm happy to say that I've been touching my toes for years. It took a lot of work, but I accomplished it; one inch at a time. I still can't whistle though, but that's okay, I can yell loudly.

What is it?
In my opinion, stretching is one of the components of fitness that is overlooked by 80% of the people who exercise. They will run for an hour, and perhaps stretch for 2 minutes. They will lift weights for an hour, and maybe stretch for 5 minutes. Don't get me wrong, stretching for 2 minutes is much better than not stretching at all. But, if that is all a person does every time, the body will start getting tighter and tighter and soon enough, something will get pulled out of place and pain will set in. That's not fun for anyone to experience.

41

Why does it matter?

So, what's the difference between stretching and flexibility?

Stretching is a very natural and instinctive thing that we humans do; you probably stretch when you first wake up in the morning. If we look at our fur babies, they stretch as soon as they wake up from a nap; we could learn a lot from them.

My definition of **flexibility** is the range of motion, or movement, around a particular joint or set of joints. In layman's terms, how far we can reach, bend or turn. When improving flexibility is the goal, the muscles, and their *fascia should be the primary focus of flexibility training.

*Fascia is a very thin sheath of connective tissue that looks much like a dense spider web. It surrounds and interconnects muscles, bones, and internal organs.

How do you do it?

There are many ways to stretch, but the two methods I mainly teach are Dynamic Stretching and Static Stretching.

DYNAMIC STRETCHING

When warming up the body **before** exercise, dynamic stretching is what you should be doing. This form of stretching is stretching with movement and it will get your body prepared for your sporting activity. To warm up the body, you want to mimic the moves you will be creating in your sport. For example, if you are a golfer, a dynamic stretch for you to do would be a gentle rotation exercise with your upper body to create the motion of swinging the club before hitting the ball.

Performing the progressive movements for a minimum of 5 minutes will increase blood flow to areas that are going to be working. The benefits include enhancing your performance, feeling more energized, improving the range of motion throughout your body, and not being tired before you even start. Be careful not to bounce or create jerking movements as this can send the wrong message to your nervous system and increase the chance of injury.

ACTIVITY	DYNAMIC STRETCHES*
Walking	Leg Swings, Calf Raises, Trunk Twists
Jogging	Leg Swings, Forward Lunges
Cycling	Leg Swings, Calf Raises, Standing Knee Hugs
Strength Training – Upper Body Option: Completing the 1st set of exercise with a light weight	Arm Circles, Trunk Twists, Shoulder Blade Squeezes, Wall Pushups
Strength Training – Lower Body Option: Completing the 1st set of exercise with a light weight	Forward and Reverse Lunges, Calf Raises, Knee Hugs
Curling	Leg Swings, Trunk Twists
Swimming	Jumping Jacks, Arm Circles, Trunk Twists

*The proper technique of the preceding dynamic stretches can be viewed at www.rhonaparsons.com/21ways

STATIC STRETCHING

This form of stretching is a holding stretch. We want to put our body in a specific position that will work on releasing tightness and will lengthen our muscles. If your body is relaxing in the stretch, you can stay there for as long as it feels good. Some holding stances though, need the contraction of the opposing muscle(s) to support the muscles that are being lengthened.

A great example is the Crescent Moon Pose shown on page 46. Some people think that they are stretching the Psoas (also known as the hip flexor) in this standing pose. The Psoas is being lengthened, not stretched (does my body look relaxed in the photo?) so the buttocks muscles (the glutes) have to be contracted to support the pelvis. The Psoas loves to be lengthened, but it is working (not relaxing) to hold us in this balanced position; therefore, it needs the support of the glutes.

YOGA

Yoga has been around for about five thousand years. It is a system that focuses on attaining self-realization and is made up of 8 limbs or pathways that take us to this realization. One of these limbs is known as ASANA. In Sanskrit, asana means 'posture' or 'pose' and is the physical portion of Yoga.

There are many different styles of asana, but the one that is known by most is Hatha Yoga. This style of asana connects breath with movement, keeping you in the present moment while you are moving through the postures. It is also the path toward creating a balance of opposites. The word Hatha is broken down to translate as Ha = sun and tha = moon. When you are in a posture, you are looking to find the balance between the effort and ease of the pose.

There are many benefits to a Hatha Yoga practice:
- The increase of strength and flexibility
- Improvement of balance and core strength
- Development of mindfulness
- Relief of chronic pain
- Aid in digestion
- Reduction of anxiety and depression
- Improvement of sleep and quality of life

Hatha Yoga can be both dynamic (e.g., Ashtanga, Power, Flow) and static (e.g., Yin, Restorative), so it is best to find the right teacher to help you choose the right class for your needs.

The following seven poses on pages 46-48 create length in the body. Take your time with each pose and if time permits, hold the position for as long as it feels good.

STANDING REACH

Side body; place foot behind the other, reach arm up and over as you push out hip

CRESCENT MOON

Hip and front of body: Step back with one foot, hip-width apart. Tighten buttocks and reach same-side arm up and back.

CHEST OPENER

HAMSTRING LENGTHENER

Chest: Step through a doorway with hands approx. shoulder height. Keep back heel down as you lean in through the doorway

Back of thigh: Set up as shown, shoulders relaxed. As you push down front heel, lift buttocks up towards ceiling

SIDELYING BOW POSE

Front of thigh, chest and shoulder: Set up as shown. Bend bottom leg for balance. Bring knee forward and grab ankle. Slowly pull leg back and line up knee with front of hip. Roll shoulder back and open chest

CAT/COW   TWISTED CAT

Back: Place hands above slightly bent knees. Tuck tail under as you round your back

Take right hand to outside of left thigh. Stabilize feet and "pull" to the right, keeping right hand attached to left thigh. Repeat on other side

DOWNWARD CAT

Animals always stretch when they first wake up.

SURROUND YOURSELF WITH POSITIVE PEOPLE

"You are the average of the five people you
spend the most time with."

Jim Rohn

What is it?

No matter who we are, we are significantly influenced by the people we hang out with and sometimes, that's not the best thing for us. The example I can give you was when my girls were in high school; they would often come home with the attitudes from all their friends. I'm sure you can relate if you have had or have teenager daughters. When I had enough of the attitude, I would sometimes ground one of them for a few days, just long enough so I could get back my daughter and enjoy who she was.

Why does it matter?

The Negative Nellie vs. the Devil's Advocate

Do you know the difference? Do you have one of those friends who never says anything positive about anyone? The person whose energy can drain you and brings nothing but pessimism into your life? This is your negative Nellie friend. How about the friend who always looks at both sides of the 'coin'? This person drives you crazy because he/she always speak of both the negative and positive. Say hello to your Devil's Advocate friend.

There is a difference between these two types of people, and while it's idyllic to be surrounded by positive, supportive people, I think we need a couple of the devil's advocates around us to keep us real. Let's face it, life isn't all about roses and butterflies, and if we want to fulfill our dreams and make our desires come to fruition, we need someone to make us look at both the good and the not so good.

Our behaviour starts to get affected though when we surround ourselves with too many negative Nellies. Our way of thinking and our decisions change and, sometimes, our self-esteem starts to go on a downward spiral! Can you think of anyone in your inner and outer circles that fit this description? Write the name(s) down.

_____ _____

We need to keep in mind that we don't get to choose our family, but we do get to choose our friends and who we want to surround ourselves with. Is there anyone that you need to reconsider whether you want them in your life?

I believe that friendships shouldn't be work. The people you choose as your friends should love you for who you are. There should be no judgement, no lies, no anger; only happiness, encouragement, support and love. If you have a friend who brings more negativity to your friendship and your life, you may want to consider loving them from afar and keeping them at arm's length. People do come into our lives for a reason, season or lifetime. They come to learn from us or for us to learn from them. Sometimes, friendships end for no other reason than when there's nothing else to give one another.

How do you do it?

Be who you are! Radiate positivity! When you begin to surround yourself with positive people, those contrary, pessimistic people will gradually disappear out of your life. Did they bring something to your life? They did, so thank them for what they brought, wish them well and let them go.

Notes

LET GO OF JUDGEMENT OF YOURSELF AND OTHERS

What is it?

Judgement is when we consciously make insulting remarks about another person or ourselves. Judgement is usually unkind and, as far as I'm concerned, a waste of time and energy. Don't get me wrong; I was as guilty as the next person. The good news is that I recognized this a long time ago and I have worked hard over the years at being non-judgemental to others, and especially to myself.

I know that we all are doing our best to live each day, and I'm pretty sure not one of us decides to screw up our life intentionally. Sometimes we are dealt specific cards, and it is up to each one of us to seek help when needed or to help others who are in need. Most people, including you and me, are doing the best they can with what they have in that particular moment. No one wakes up and says, "I think I'll screw up my life today." Give yourself, and others, a break.

When you judge other people, you are putting negative energy into your heart, which resonates out into the world. Have you heard the words 'misery loves company'? Have you been in a group setting when a person starts to gossip about another, and everyone gets in on the conversation? People feed off each other, and this is how mean-spirited groups form. The thing is, we rarely ever walk in another's shoes; we know that they don't fit into ours so there must be something wrong with them or their actions. I've been on the end of gossip many times, and I remember how hurt I felt, how sad it made me feel because I thought those people were my friends.

When we can let go of what others think of us, we create freedom for ourselves! I have no control over what others think of me. I do have the power, however, how I respond to their words by my actions.

Can you think of a time when you were with someone who started to gossip about another? What was your reaction? Did you contribute to the judgement or did you throw in a positive attribute to the conversation? Write the positive attribute here:

_____

_____

_____

Why does it matter?

I believe that judgement signifies a lack of self-acceptance as well; you are at war with yourself. Have you heard of 'mirroring'? Mirroring is a self-image of what we see in others. We see our bad traits, things that we don't like about ourselves in others. These behaviours can show up as our insecurities and our weaknesses. Once you can wrap your head around this, you can start to bring about changes in yourself.

How do you do it?

- Observe your thoughts
- Quit comparing yourself to others
- Develop self-acceptance by letting go of judgements that don't serve you
- Train your mind to see the good in others and yourself
- Remove yourself from any gossiping circles
- Inject positive attributions when someone begins to judge another
- Practice positive self-talk by writing affirmations

An affirmation is a great way to invoke positive thoughts in your mind. Here are some examples: I am happy and grateful now that I... "Am the creator of my world," "love me!", "am non-judgemental to myself and others," "let go of all the lies I tell myself."

Write your affirmation here and practice saying it daily:

_____

_____

_____

_____

You can download an affirmation card from my website: www.rhonaparsons.com/21ways. Make many copies; carry one with you and place others around your home, so you have constant reminders of your new way of thinking. Believe it, and you will achieve it!

MONEY MAKES THE WORLD GO AROUND!

What is it?

What is your money story? What emotions, judgements, and values do you have about money? How do these set of beliefs affect your investment in your health and wellness?

Money is thought of in many ways by people's opinions and their relationship with it. There is a vast spectrum of people's attitudes between ABUNDANCE and INSUFFICIENCY. Some people believe that it can buy you happiness. While I agree that you can do a lot of things when you have money, I don't think that it can buy you happiness. (Read more about happiness in Chapter 15). Money can buy you all the materialistic things you desire. However, when you don't have any money to buy even the basics, especially when you have a family depending on you, it can be extremely stressful and can create an inner struggle of doubt and sometimes despair.

Have you ever given it any thought about how money was considered by your parents and others around you when you were growing up? Your attitude and beliefs around money were unconsciously embedded in your mind at a young age. I learned that money was evil and that without it you would be poor and therefore, you couldn't be happy.

My parents worked very hard at giving us a great childhood, but they fought about money all the time (it seemed). There was never enough. I can only imagine how stressful this was for them; trying to build a life for themselves, my three siblings and me.

Why does it matter?

By understanding your values and attitudes toward money, you will start to see it in a very different light - the light of energy. I have learned that money is meant to flow, going from one to another through an exchange. When you start to understand that money in, and money out makes up this energy exchange, you will begin to gain control of how you spend money instead of it controlling you.

I always struggled with the way I handled money. I was forever in debt it seemed, but I never spent frivolously, notably when I was a single Mum with three little girls, ages 2, 4 and 6. Mum and Dad helped a lot by bringing groceries over, taking the girls for sleepovers, swimming, dance lessons, and even on vacations. I never bought myself clothes or splurged to get my hair done, but I always struggled to make ends meet and had to juggle the money I did have. If I had an electricity bill to pay one month but needed to buy the girls much-needed shoes, I would buy the shoes and pay the minimum amount due on the electricity bill. I could never get ahead and this juggling habit carried on for years.

It wasn't until 2012 when I became physically, mentally, and emotionally drained, and had a nervous breakdown, that I knew things had to change. From all the stress in my life, my adrenal glands were depleted. I had no strength in my body to move and no energy to worry about anything. I began to look at all the aspects of my life, and I realized one major stressor was my relationship with money; I needed to start over and begin a friendship with it. I needed to learn how to have a trusting relationship with it.

How do you do it?

1. I began looking back on my childhood and remembered how Mum and Dad related to money. It made so much sense to me when I compared how Mum and Dad always reacted around it and how I did too; it was the same way. What are your childhood memories of your parents' relationship with money?

_____

_____

_____

_____

2. I began to understand my worries and wishes. I was always putting out great vibrations to attract abundance in wealth, but in the next thought, I was putting out the negative waves of never having enough money. My positive thought was aways "I am financially wealthy and debt free" but then a little while later, worry would set in, and my next thought would be "I have no money to pay my bills!" I was inviting more money into my life, but I was also asking for no money to pay my bills.

What I have learned from reading many books on attracting all that you desire in to your life, is that you can't think both positive and negative thoughts. To create  change, you have to think only positive thoughts, and when considering these thoughts, you have to feel them too; deep inside, feeling the sense of gratitude and belief that you already have what you desire. This way of thinking is called the LAW OF ATTRACTION. Many books speak of this law; *Think and Grow Rich* by Napoleon Hill, and *The Law of Attraction* by Esther and Jerry Hicks are two of my favourites.

3. I began to meditate for 10-15 minutes every morning. **Try it.** For a few minutes every day, find a quiet place where you can sit, close your eyes and begin to relax. Once you are comfortable, imagine the inside of  your eyelids like a movie screen and on that screen, visualize EVERYTHING you desire. See your perfect home, the new car, sharing your gifts with the world, financial

wealth and independence, the ideal family life, serving others.

Use your five senses to see your new bank account balance, smell the leather of the new car, hear the delightful giggles of the children you're building a school for in Ecuador, taste the delicious food cooking in your new kitchen, and touch the petals of the beautiful flowers growing in the garden at your new cottage. The more you can connect with all that you desire, the more these ideas will become your reality.

My Dad described the difference between thinking and meditating to me and he used electricity as an example. When we are just thinking about new ideas and all that we desire, we're using about 120 volts of charge; this is the amount of electricity that your iron and kettle use. But when we are thinking of all the same things through meditation for 10-15 minutes every day, we supercharge the power to 220 volts; the energy needed to run your stove and washing machine. Do you see how powerful meditating can be? Believe it and eventually you will receive it.

4. I started to put away 10% of my monthly earnings. I learned that we must pay ourself first, so I have a certain amount taken out of my bank account bi-weekly

and put into a savings account. My motto is "out of sight, out of mind."

5. I have created a budget so now I always know where my money is being spent and no longer worry about not having enough.

6. When I see something I would like to buy, I ask the question "do I need it or do I want it?" This question has helped me from not spending money on frivolous purchases, and it has also helped me enjoy buying the things that bring me joy that I can afford.

7. If I have a particular set goal in mind, a vacation or a fitness conference, for example, I have to decide if I want to put the money towards my vacation for spending or do I buy the shoes? Now if I'm buying the shoes for the holiday I will probably buy them. A girl can never have too many pairs of shoes!

Notes

GOAL SETTING

"If you fail to plan, you plan to fail."
Benjamin Franklin

What is it?
Goal setting is a potent tool for helping you create all that you desire in your life. We all have goals whether it is to lose 20 pounds, buy a vacation home in Mexico, or get out of debt. You can use this tool to motivate yourself to turn your vision of this future into reality.

Why does it matter?
Why is it important to set goals for yourself? Setting goals gives you motivation and something to strive for. It helps you create a time management plan, explore your resources so that you can achieve the goals you are aiming for, and know what actions you need to take to bring your goals to fruition.

Goal setting is an important method of deciding what you want to achieve in your life. By writing it down, and then figuring out the steps to help you get you there. A great acronym to use when creating goals is the **SMART** acronym:

S = Specific. "I want to lose weight." is not a precise goal and only wishful thinking. It becomes a goal when it's changed to "I will lose 10 pounds in 90 days."

M = Measurable. If a goal cannot be measured, you won't accomplish it because you have no way of measuring your progress.

A = Achievable. The goal should be out of reach enough to be challenging, but it should not be out of sight.

R = Realistic. The goal has to be realistic for it to come to fruition. A person who wants to lose 50 pounds in 30 days is being unrealistic.

T = Time-bound. There should always be a starting date and a finishing date for a goal.

A man was travelling and stopped at an intersection.
He asked an elderly man, "Where does this road take me?"
The elderly person asked, "Where do you want to go?"
The man replied, "I don't know."
The elderly person said "Then take any road.
What difference does it make?"
Unknown

How accurate is that quote? When we don't know where we are going, it doesn't matter which road we take. Goals without actions are empty dreams. The steps that we take turn dreams into goals. Even if we miss our goals, it doesn't make us a failure. Delay doesn't mean defeat. It only means that we have to create another plan to accomplish our target.

How do you do it?
If you ask most people what their one primary objective is in life, they would possibly give you an unclear answer, such as, "I want to be successful", "I want to be happy", or "I want to make a good living," Unfortunately, all three of these objectives are only wishes and dreams; none of them are clear goals.

So what steps do you need to take to make your dreams and goals become your reality? You need to figure out your BHAG. BHAG? This great acronym stands for "Big Hairy Audacious Goals" that authors James Collins and Jerry Porras wrote about in their 1994 book *"Built to Last: Successful Habits of Visionary Companies."* Your BHAG should give you butterflies in your belly; those feelings of excitement that give you the power to make those goals happen.

1. To help you figure out your goals, use the form on page 69 to write down ten BHAG that you want to achieve within the next three years, and then choose three goals that you want to accomplish this year. This task can be challenging; however, focus on the ones that are achievable and the ones that are going to keep you on your path to the larger goal. Choosing specific

goals will allow you to concentrate easily on them and bring focus to the task at hand.

2. You now need to figure out the resources that will help you achieve your goals. Brainstorm what you believe are the most critical resources that will help you reach your target. Do you need to research a specific subject? Is there a mentor or coach that can help you? Is there a course you need to take to get the certification or position you are wanting? This step is vital to get you on your way to creating success and will help you visualize what you need to do to make your dream come to fruition.

3. This next step is the most important of all. It doesn't matter how many resources you have, without action nothing will happen. You must act! What radical actions do you need to take and that are required to get you to stay on schedule? If this seems overwhelming, you may want to break your actions down into individual tasks, or smaller goals, so that you know what you need to do each day to stay on schedule.

Make three copies of the individual goal sheet on page 70 and write down your BHAG and begin planning your future! Remember to use the SMART approach. If you don't want to use the goal list and goal setting sheet in the book, you can download them at www.rhonaparsons.com/21ways.

Remember, to achieve your goals you need to stay organized and stay on top of the tasks required. Focus on what you need to do every month, each week, and every day this year to reach your broader goals, and then get started. Good luck!

> *A DREAM written down with a date becomes a GOAL*
> *A goal broken down into steps becomes a PLAN*
> *A plan backed by ACTION makes your dreams into*
> *REALITY...*
> *Greg Reid*

10 BHAG I WILL ACCOMPLISH IN THE NEXT 3 YEARS

1.	
2.	
3.	
4.	
5.	
6.	
7.	
8.	
9.	
10.	

GOAL:

TARGET DATE OF COMPLETION:

RESOURCES:

1._____

2._____

3._____

4._____

RADICAL ACTIONS:

1._____

2._____

3._____

4._____

LET GO OF THE PAST; BE PRESENT

*"The present moment is the only moment available to us,
and it is the door to all moments."*
                                    Thich Nhat Hanh

What is it?
Being present is about simplifying life. It's about living in the moment and letting go of things that are out of our control. It's about not thinking of what has happened in the past or worrying about the future. The past as we know it is gone; we cannot bring it back, it can't be changed. The future is only an illusion, and when we continuously keep focusing on the tomorrow, we are missing the moments of right now.

Why does it matter?
Bringing up memories of the past can never help us move forward in life. Old feelings of things that have happened in the past can ruin the present moment and, unfortunately, we all do this unconsciously. There are so many triggers out in the world

that can bring up old feelings and snap us right out of the present moment.

I'd like you to take a moment and visualize your heart as an onion with many layers. See it with all its layers and each layer representing an experience, good or bad, that has happened to you over your lifetime. Many of our day-to-day experiences are merely that, experiences, and these flow through us continuously as they appear. However, we also have had those experiences that made a significant impact on us. Those moments that made us very happy ("that was the most beautiful kiss; I'll never forget it as long as I live!"), the very sad moments ("I can't believe my boyfriend dumped me because I wouldn't have sex with him"), and the angry, frustrated moments too. These are the layers on the heart. All those moments have stuck to our heart, much like the layers of an onion.

Our heart is covered in these layers, these good and bad memories, which have happened to us in our lifetime. We have held onto these experiences and, as long as these layers are on our heart, we are always going to react when a memory is triggered. Let me give you an example:

A friend of mine, let's call her Judy, was quite chunky growing up and was always ridiculed by a few kids at school. They would call her names, one in particular when she would walk by them in the hallway or outside. Each time she heard the name, her self-esteem got cut into pieces. It was years later when Judy was joking around with her boyfriend and, responding to something she had said; he jokingly called her the very same name that had hurt her years before. Immediately she felt this horrible gut feeling, and all those crappy memories came back in an instant. She could feel the fear and the sadness instantly in her body, and once again her self-esteem dropped to a deep empty feeling that surged through her. How awful for her!

When we focus only on the past and what has transpired from those fears that we have held onto unconsciously, our future can be destroyed. The same can be said by worrying about things that "might happen" because this can keep us in a state of anxiety and fear.

How do you do it?
So, what can you do to get rid of these things that are pulling you down and not allowing you to live the life that you want to live, living life to the fullest in the present moment?

As I've said before, awareness is the beginning of change. Begin to recognize the memories that push your buttons and bring up all those fears; this is the first step to peeling those layers off of your heart. To free your heart from these burdens is the best gift you can give yourself. Releasing these layers from your subconscious mind and your heart will put a stop to the feelings of sadness, anger, frustration or low self-esteem.

Can you think of any memories that bring up feelings of fear, sadness, and anger?

_____

_____

_____

_____

When my hubby was sick, I learned very quickly to stay present in every moment even though I wasn't dealing with any of the stress that was building. I couldn't even think about the future, the 'ifs' of what could transpire. I needed to be 100% in the moment for both of us. I could only function living in the moment, focusing on what needed to be done for him and us right there and then. I was looking after him and the household and also working full time in a management position at a local fitness studio.

I had a team of 15 amazing instructors that needed my guidance and expertise to run the group fitness department with ease and proficiency. I had no time to get lost in the past or future. There was work to be done, and a lot of people were relying on me. If it weren't for those incredible women and my wonderful colleague, Kathy, I would have crumbled so fast and would not have been able to help anyone – let alone myself.

After my hubby started on his journey of recovery, I finally had time for me. From reading many self-care books, I realized I needed to help myself get over those feelings of sadness, etc. and I began to recognize when an awful feeling would start to stir at my emotions and begin to raise its ugly head. I would take time and go to a quiet place somewhere, sit down and begin focusing on my breath.

When we breathe in and out through our nose, a relaxation response is created. I visualized me sitting on top of my heart in a cross-legged position and saw the layer of disruption covering my heart. My goal was to peel that layer right off, to discard the burden it was carrying within its folds.

Every time I went to this place of emotional stress; I had two choices:

1. To feel the emotion and dive right off my heart into the ocean of the feeling, spluttering, drowning and eventually dragging myself back on top of my heart; the sentiment attaching itself stronger onto my heart, or

2. Instead of diving into those same feelings, I allowed the emotions to flow freely through my heart so that it did not get stuck as another layer. I may have spilled a few tears, but they were tears of release.

It only took a couple of times before I was able to free the burden that had become part of my belief system. Yes, I had many layers to get rid of, but each time it got a little more comfortable. When I needed a little help on emotions that were stuck, I would book an appointment with my coach, and she would help me release the memory that no longer served me.

Try the following practice the next time you feel an emotion that isn't serving you coming up to the surface.

1. Go to a quiet place where you won't be disturbed by someone; turn off your electronics. Sit in a comfortable position and take a big breath in and out.

2. Begin practicing the **Complete Breath Technique** (found in Chapter 1) to bring you to a place of calmness. Take a few minutes to quieten your mind and relax your body.

3. When you are ready, bring the emotion to the front of your thoughts and notice where you feel the angst in your body. Focus on how your body is reacting to it; let the tears of release flow and feel the burden of your emotion getting smaller and eventually releasing.

Close your eyes. Clear your heart. Let it go.

BE GRATEFUL

"Gratitude is the rich soil to start growing amazing things!"

What is it?

Gratitude is the next step toward your healing and bringing balance to your life. Being grateful for all that you have is imperative to living a healthy emotional stress-free life. Along with gratitude comes happiness; be grateful and feel it in your heart. Feeling it in your heart will bring joy to you and inevitably, will be felt by those closest to you.

Be grateful for the insight that you will experience through this process of acknowledgment of the emotion and in letting go. Letting go means releasing this burden to a higher authority; allow the healing process to begin. This is the time to put the burden down, step over it, and move through your day with a lighter step, clarity, and trust that you are looked after by a loving field of energy. Letting go of the burden is mighty. We must acknowledge the pain of the emotion and fully experience the feeling without judgement or attachment. Know that gratitude is a fantastic tool to move the negative energy into healing you. Letting go of negativity helps us fear less and love more.

Why does it matter?

Gratitude is an excellent tool to move negative energy, replacing it with peace and love. When we can truly love our self, fear will begin to dissipate, and we will start to experience inner peace. We are all here to experience love and peace. However, to experience these two beautiful feelings, we have first to experience fear and disharmony. It is the Ying and Yang of life. All is duality; it is only love or fear.

How do you do it?

1. Begin to cultivate and consciously apply an attitude of gratitude every day.

2. Start by creating a gratitude journal. Writing in a journal brings your feelings to fruition and something you can look back at whenever you need some inspiration. I write my appreciations in a journal and, as well, on an affirmation card that I always keep with me. My card not only has all the things that I already have

written on it but the things that I also desire in my life. When I read out loud from my card, as if I already have them, I am aligning myself with my goals and desires.

Use the card below or download an affirmation card from my website: www.rhonaparsons.com/21ways

What are you grateful for in your life? Write it here:

AFFIRMATION CARD

I am so happy and so grateful now that I have:

_____

_____

_____

_____

_____

---

1. Choose the same time every day to acknowledge and express appreciation for where you are in your life and for what you have; your home, career, car, family.

2. Write with heartfelt gratitude and feel the emotions that come up.

3. Before you go to sleep at night, think of three things that you are grateful for that have made you happy during the day. Be thankful for those things and feel them in your heart.

Be generous with gratitude, for it is contagious.

"If you feel happy for what you have, have an attitude of gratitude and be grateful.,. then it will come true, and you will be great, and you will be full!

Yogi Bajan

FOCUS ON THE GOOD

*"When you change the way you look at things,
the things you look at will change."*
Wayne Dyer

What is it?

Focusing on the good things in your life is a sure way to find appreciation for all you have. Each day, through self-care, I am growing and finding out more about whom I am, always digging deeper and then sharing what I learn. When we can start to appreciate all that we have, to find joy in all that surrounds the people who are in our lives and us, we will see that life is excellent.

Why does it matter?

Unfortunately, we are bombarded daily with the unpleasantries in our life too. The cranky boss, the continuous rainy days, or the dog across the street that never stops barking. Even the news on TV is 99% unenjoyable. It is so easy for us to be pulled in to all of the negative things that are going on around us. If we can start to see the glitter amongst the rocks, life will become so much more pleasant and enjoyable for us and those around us. There needs to be more focus on the good in this world, and the best way we can do this is to start at home.

How do you do it?

How do we begin to see the good in everything? We need to look at everything as Ying and Yang; the universal symbol of balance and harmony. This symbol reminds us that life is all about balancing the good with the bad, the joys and the challenges, the ups, and downs. It also tells us that there is always a brighter side to everything; it's up to us to look for it and focus on that rather than the negative.

If we break apart the Ying/Yang symbol, we see both a dark side and a light side. The dark side represents the bad, and the light side represents the good. But inside the dark there is light, and on the light side, there is dark. When these two sides are connected, they create life as we know it. You see, without knowing darkness, we can't know light. Without knowing bad, we can't know good. Without knowing sadness, we can't know joy. Both sides of the symbol are dependent on the other to create a whole.

When my daughter sits down at the table with her family every evening for supper, each family member takes turns talking about the thorns and roses of their day. The thorns represent something that happened that didn't make them feel happy, and the rose represents the good that happened. I experienced this conversation one evening, and it brought joy to my heart to hear my grandchildren tell us of their day, to be able to distinguish the difference between happy and sad and to know what they could do to turn their experience of the thorn in to a better experience.

I'm sure you already have ways to bring good into your life but here are a few ideas that can bring even more joy to you.

1. Stop what you are doing, look around you and write down two things you see that make you feel good.

    _____

    _____

2. Write down the names of three people who bring joy in to your life. Phone one of them and set up a date for a visit.

_____

_____

_____

3. Write down three good things that happened yesterday that made you feel great. Notice the joy you feel in your heart when you are writing it down.

_____

_____

_____

4. Think of something that has happened recently that was a thorn in your side. Now write down the rose that came out of your experience.

_____

_____

_____

5. Express gratitude to those who have made a difference in your life. Send a card. Write a letter. Make a phone call. Visit in person.

6.Simplify life by decluttering and letting go of things that cause you stress.

7. End each day thinking about three things that you are grateful for that happened during the day. Feel the gratitude in your heart and then say each thing out loud with a smile on your face and love in your heart.

Notes

LET GO OF THINGS YOU CANNOT CHANGE

*Dear self: don't get worked up over things you can't
change or people you can't change. It's not worth
the anger built up or the heartache.
Control only what you can. Let go. Love Me*

What is it?

"IT IS WHAT IT IS" These simple words are a truth-seeking statement. When something is out of our control, these words bring the situation to fruition. It is neither negative nor positive; it just IS.

Why does it matter?

When we can recognize and come to terms with "it is what it is" in any given situation, we can immediately let go of all expectations and set ourselves free, allowing us to move forward with courage, no judgement, and a complete understanding of what IS. Let go of things you have no control over. When we realize that what is happening to other people, or what others think of us is none of our business, life becomes so much lighter.

How do you do it?
The following excerpt is by an unknown author.

Below are instructions on how to let go. Perhaps it is letting go of a rebellious child, or a burden of sorrow, losing a loved one or learning to live with a heartache which we just cannot let go. Read this over, study it, pray over it and you will find that letting go will release peace within you, which will allow your spirit to soar, to be free. Give entirely to your Divine and let the work be done within you where the need is anyway.

LETTING GO

*To let go doesn't mean to stop caring,
it means I can't do it for someone else.*

*To let go is not to cut myself off,
it's the realization that I can't control another.*

*To let go is not to enable,
but to allow learning from natural consequences.*

*To let go is to admit powerlessness,
which means the outcome is not in my hands.*

*To let go is not to try to change or blame another,
I can only change myself.*

To let go is not to care for, but to care about.

To let go is not to fix, but to be supportive.
To let go is not to judge,
but to allow another to be a human being.

To let go is not to be in the middle arranging all the outcomes,
but to allow others to affect their own outcomes.

To let go is not to be protective,
it is to permit another to face reality.

To let go is not to deny, but to accept.

To let go is not to nag, scold or argue,
but to search out my own shortcomings and to correct them.

To let go is not to adjust everything to my desires,
but to take each day as it comes and to cherish the moment.

To let go is not to criticize and regulate anyone,
but to try to become what I dream I can be.

To let go is not to regret the past,
but to grow and live for the future.

To let go is to fear less and love more.

Author Unknown

Do you have something on your mind that you want to let go of? Here's the perfect spot to do it. Write away! ♥

_____

_____

_____

_____

_____

_____

_____

BE HAPPY

What is it?

The pursuit of happiness and how to live life to the fullest. Sounds awesome right? Do you want to live that way? Live your life to the fullest so that you can enjoy every day? I'm sure your answer is yes; it's mine too, and I am trying my hardest to do that. I would like to share with you some of the things that I've learned over the years and hope to inspire you on how you can live your life to the fullest too and experience true happiness.

Happiness comes from our heart; it comes from within, and I think a lot of people tend to look externally for happiness. Happiness is a state of well-being that encompasses living a good life. To achieve happiness, it involves a time of substantial discomfort. You see, to get to the place of joy, we need to first experience all the other emotions on the other end of the spectrum: anger, frustration, fear, resentment, judgements, grief, guilt, control, inadequacy, abandonment, and more. We need to understand that we need to go to the lows to experience the highs.

Why does it matter?

I read recently that many of us today live safer and are wealthier and healthier than previous generations, but we are more miserable than ever before. I believe this is because we don't live by the minimalist approach. People need to have stuff nowadays and surround themselves with the best of everything, but more and more, people realize that all this 'stuff' doesn't bring pure happiness and joy into their lives. Sadly, this is adding to the misery so many people are living with today in our world.

How do you do it?

What are your past-time passions? What are some things that make you happy? What do you love to do?

I love to work in my garden, I love to hang out with my hubby and friends, and I love being around my grandchildren and my daughters. These things make me smile and fill up my happiness tank. I try to do them as often as I can. Write your happy things here:

_____

_____

_____

Do you enjoy what you do every day? Many of us work long hours daily, so your job needs to be something that you are very passionate about. I can honestly tell you that every day I get up (and that makes me happy) I am excited to go to work because I love sharing my work and I love helping people live the best lives they can. Are you passionate about your career or your day-to-day life? Yes? Great!

No? What can you do to bring joy and fulfillment in to your day?

_____

_____

_____

Simplify your life. Sometimes we can have way too many things on our schedule, and too much of anything can cause stress and decrease our happiness. Is there anything that you can eliminate from your life to ease the burden?

_____

_____

_____

I hope this has given you some insight into how you can bring more happiness to the surface because there's always more for us, after all, we are made up of pure joy and happiness.

We are here to experience life. We have the choice to either live our life to the fullest or not. Our thoughts and emotions come from only one of two places – fear or love.

You have two choices: be happy or not...what do you choose?

I CHOOSE_____

"The way to happiness is: keep your heart free from hate,
your mind from worry. Live simply, give much.
Fill your life with love. Do as you would be done by."
                                        Buddha

SPEAK AND LIVE YOUR TRUTH

"If you tell the truth, you don't have to
remember anything"
Mark Twain

What is it?

As far as I am concerned, speaking and living your truth should be everyone's number one value. It was a belief that was ingrained in me growing up and one that I'm grateful for having. Telling the truth, or being honest, is not only about being true to you but also to the other person/people that are involved in the conversation. I am sure you've heard the quote "Honesty is the best policy"; it's all about telling the truth.

Have you ever had someone lie to you? Have you been caught in a lie? I'm sure we have all told at least one 'little white lie' in our lifetime. This is typically because we don't want to hurt another person's feelings. Or, in the case of when I was a little girl and told a lie, not wanting to get into trouble from the consequences that would happen if I was caught lying. Sooner or later though, the truth would be revealed, and that little white lie would come back and bite me in the you-know-what! Honesty and truthfulness are not just about telling the truth; it is a way of life.

Why does it matter?
My father instilled fear in me about lying when I was growing up. If I lied and got caught, I felt the wrath of his hand on my behind; luckily I only remember one incident. It was enough never to lie again. It's probably the reason that I had zero tolerance for lying when my daughters were growing up. I always told them that telling the truth would have fewer consequences than lying to me. Of course, their punishment was usually in the form of grounding them from seeing their friends. It's funny how we typically lie to the ones we love the most!

If we can't be true to our self, it's pretty hard being true to others. So why is lying an immoral thing to do? I believe that it comes down to our values. Lying creates mistrust between people. One of my values is integrity and with that comes all of the other values that you see on page 98.

Whenever I have to confront someone and speak my truth that he/she may not agree with, I take my time creating the right dialogue. I first ask myself three questions:

Is it true? Is it kind? Is it necessary?

You see, I want to get my truth across in the kindest possible way and for me to move forward it is necessary that I do it. From past experiences, if I don't speak my truth, the emotion will eventually begin to fester in me, and I know that anger will start to rear its ugly head. Then when I express my truth, it ain't pretty! If my words are not expressed with kindness and compassion to the other person, they can come across as mean and hurtful and can create a landslide of hurt feelings for him/her.

How do you do it?
What are your values?

_____

_____

_____

_____

_____

_____

_____

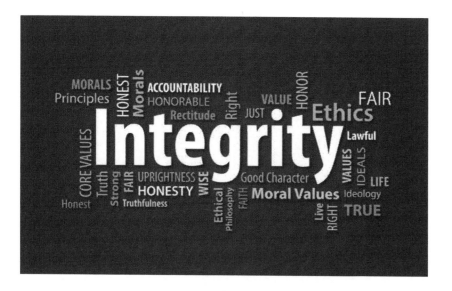

Always speak from your heart because the truth will forever set you free. 💜

FORGIVE

True forgiveness is when you can say
"thank you for that experience."
Oprah Winfrey

What is it?

According to the Merriam Webster Dictionary, the definition for FORGIVE is to stop feeling anger toward someone who has done something wrong, to stop blaming someone, to stop feeling angry about something, and to forgive someone for something wrong. Forgiveness is a process that we go through after another has wronged us. It is when we choose to let go of the anger and resentment and replace it with compassion.

A few years ago, I had a friend who I liked very much; let's call her Jane. She began as a client of mine, and our friendship grew over time. We started to spend quite a bit of time together outside the gym: going for walks, going for the occasional drink and we talked a lot about life and family. I appreciated her friendship.

At the end of that year, I decided to have an appreciation party for all of my clients to thank them for their support and trusting me to help them on their fitness journeys. I created the invitations on my computer and emailed the invites out. Unfortunately, only 50 email addresses could be mailed in one batch, so the last two invites went out to Jane and another gal. The other gal's email address had a connotation to it (that I was completely oblivious too) that Jane noticed. I received an awful phone call from her accusing me of ridiculing her (because of the other gal's email address!) It was ridiculous! I was distraught by the accusation and was stunned that she would think I would imply such a thing.

We didn't talk for a couple of months and then one day I was sitting outside a local cafe with my sister enjoying a cup of freshly brewed coffee. I saw Jane going into another store, I didn't shout out to say hi. I guess she saw me too because when I was home later that day, Jane called to apologize. I accepted her apology, and we decided to meet up for a walk. It was like nothing had happened, and we were back to our original relationship.

It was probably six months later that I received an email from a friend that made me laugh out loud (I'm English and have the dry British humour) so I forwarded it to all my friends so that they could laugh too. Jane was very angry when she called me and once again accused me of many things regarding the email. After trying to explain my actions to her, and her not having any openness to the email or my explanations, I was done and told her so. After hanging up, I was so mad at myself for putting me in that predicament once again. To make a long story short and many not-so-nice emails from her, I finally had to block her from my email. Over the next year, I would see her periodically in a grocery store or on the street, and she'd stop to say hi, but I had nothing to say to her, and I would leave angry (at me) each time.

Four years later Jane showed up at one of my Yoga classes. As soon as I saw her walk through the door, my heart started to beat quickly, and I felt the heat rising in me. It was different this time though; there was no anger. I had forgiven her...and in doing so, let go of the anger. I had not forgotten what she had done, but I had let it go. To this day she will still show up occasionally to class. I am always polite to her as I am to the next person and serve her with compassion and forgiveness. Do I want our friendship back? No, and I know that I am a lot better and happier without it.

Why does it matter?
Forgiveness doesn't mean that you forget about or condone the wrongdoing. You can forgive a person for their actions, but it doesn't mean that you believe that their actions were justified or acceptable. Forgiveness is an emotional change and is the first step in healing yourself and growing.

101

It is a powerful change because it releases you from holding on to some thoughts and feelings that are not serving you. The wrongdoing that you are holding on to when someone has hurt you is only a thought, but it's taking up space in your brain and your heart. When you can't forgive someone, you are holding on to that negativity, and over time you will get increasingly bitter; this feeling is giving the other person power over you. Forgiveness does not change what has happened to you in the past, but it will change your future.

Self-forgiveness is a very important step in releasing the experience and moving forward. When I think of the saying "Fool me once, shame on you, fool me twice, shame on me," I remember the times that I was made a fool of and how I felt. Each time I felt very betrayed and guilty too for allowing someone to make a fool of me, and it made me angry. It wasn't my fault, yet I took on the blame for the situation. What did I do wrong? Did I trust the person too much? Maybe it was my fault?

Have you done that? Blamed yourself for being ridiculed, laughed at, or made a fool of? Are you holding on to anger towards someone? Write your experience here:

_____

_____

_____

_____

Self-forgiveness is hard to do, but it is needed for us to let go of what another did to us and get back our power. I'm sure you'll agree with me that people who forgive others are a lot happier and healthier than those who hold on to resentments. I know that I changed once I had done the work of forgiveness towards Jane.

I believe people come into our lives for a reason, season or lifetime, either to learn from us or for us to learn from them. They will gradually disappear out of your life once the lesson has been given or learned. Did they bring something to your life? Yes they did so thank them for what they brought, wish them well and let them go.

Today, there is too much disconnection, hatred, conflict, and sadness in the world. We need to learn how to forgive and love one another freely, to recognize our self in each other and to work together to create unity in the world.

How do you do it?

"Forgiveness is just another name for freedom."
Byron Katie

When we can forgive another for their wrongdoing, we are setting ourselves free. We will no longer be tied down by their wrongdoings or by our feelings towards them. So how can we forgive another? Here are some ideas that may help you:

- Write a letter to the person who has wronged you. You don't have to give it to them but writing down your feelings can begin the healing process.

- Don't go to sleep angry. As I shared with you in Chapter 13, turn those thoughts of anger into gratitude. Look for the good in what has come out of your experience that has appeared as anger in you.

- Think about the incident with a clear mind and how it affected you. What role did you play in the scenario? Could you have reacted differently?

- Recognize that what happened had nothing to do with you. When we realize that what another person thinks of us is none of our business, healing begins immediately.

- Write down your forgiveness on a piece of paper. Begin with "I honestly and truly forgive _____(person) for _____

    _____ (the betrayal).

Write down all that you need to say. Take the paper and sit with it for a few minutes. Close your eyes and hold the paper between your hands in front of your heart. Visualize the words and say them out loud, beginning with "I honestly and truly forgive_____. When you are ready, light a match and burn the paper (in a safe place). Sit with your feelings for as long as you need to.

I promise you that by following just one or all these ideas, the feelings that you are holding on to will begin to dissolve and allow you to move forward with ease and grace. Tomorrow is a new day.

Notes

LIVE AUTHENTICALLY

*"Authenticity is a collection of choices that we get to make
every day. It's about the choice to show up and be real.
The choice to be honest. The choice to
let our true selves be seen."*
Brene Brown

What is it?

When we were babies, we were born beautiful little spirits full of love and only knew love and happiness. We didn't understand hate, and we weren't fearful of anything. We were 100% authentic. We were real.

From the age of four onwards, our belief systems began being created by learning from the people that were our tribe (Mum and Dad, sisters, cousins, brothers) and whoever else was in our life. This time was the beginning of unauthenticity.

Why does it matter?

Some of us go through the facade of life wearing a mask and being who others expect us to be. We fill up our days serving others, taking on another's opinions, and we get caught up in this crazy world that we lose sight of who we indeed are. Living your life to please others is not living authentically. You can only live up to others' expectations for so long; eventually, the mold that has been formed around you will crack and break. How can you live a happy fulfilled life when you are not doing what you want to do?

It has only been in the last five years that I have lived my life the way I want to; completely authentic. Before that, I was always trying to please everyone and live up to everyone's expectations of me. When I looked back into my past, I realized I had been living most of my life by what was expected of me from my family, managers, colleagues and some of my friends. Yes, I had made specific choices on how I was living my life, but the decisions I was making weren't coming from my heart and gut (which is where my true authenticity comes from); they were arising from expectation, fear, depression, guilt, and sadness.

In October 2010 the first crack of my mold of unauthenticity happened. For the next two years, my life was continuingly changing, and I was not happy. I was exhausted, sad, and just wanted my life to change. I had no idea what was going to happen, but something had to. One evening In August 2012, after having cried for most of the day, I sat in my hot tub, looked up at the sky and said to the Universe "I'm ready...bring it on". A week later I left my hubby and a month later, my business. I headed into an emotional/nervous breakdown. I was in a state of Adrenal Exhaustion; I was done. I couldn't help anyone with their fitness/health/wellness journeys, let alone help me, and so...I... surrendered.

Even though I was at this very dark place, I wasn't afraid because I knew I was being looked after and guided. It was where I needed to be; the Phoenix had died and was waiting to be reborn. For the next few months, after getting back on my feet, I had to make some crucial decisions because I knew that I needed to de-stress my life if I wanted happiness and fulfillment and to live by my standards; to be who I truly was.

Are there certain thoughts/beliefs/feelings that are holding you back from being authentic? Tick the ones that apply to you:

You live in the past a lot   ____

You are always trying to please others   ____

You don't think you're good enough   ____

Your cup always seems half empty   ____

You feel like you're going to explode some days   ____

You can never say no   ____

Your vocabulary is made up of a lot of 'what ifs?" ____

You always worry about what others think of you   ____

Can you think of any other thoughts/belief/feelings that are stopping you from living the life you desire?

_____

_____

_____

_____

How do you do it?

What can you do to get rid of these things that are pulling you down and not allowing you to live the life that you want to live; living life to the fullest?

1. Again, awareness is the beginning of change. Begin to recognize when something you hear or see pushes your buttons and brings up negative emotions. Sit with this for a while; contemplate your feelings and ask the questions, "what is going on here? What is the truth? Why do I feel like this?" Don't try too hard to find an answer; let the first thing that comes to mind be your guide.

2. Get rid of any negativity in your life. Do you have somebody that you work with, a member of your family, or a friend that is very pessimistic? Is their cup always half empty? They're never helpful, and

they bring you down every time they're with you? Get rid of them! Stop hanging out with them and start hanging out with your positive friends and meet new people. Those negative people in your life will begin to disappear; they'll stop calling, and they'll stop showing up.

3. As mentioned in Chapter 13, gratitude is an easy way to begin feeling happy. Be grateful for things that are happening in your life and always feel them in your heart.

4. What are your past-time passions? What makes you happy? What do you love to do? Write down your past-time passions here.

_____

_____

_____

_____

5. Live an authentic and meaningful life. Be true to yourself and live in line with your values. Ask yourself:
Who am I?

_____

What do I want in life?

_____

Am I true to who I am?

_____

What small steps can I take to move in the direction of living life to the fullest; to be my true authentic self?

_____

_____

_____

_____

LIVE YOUR DREAM

What is it?

Living your dream means to be active in your life and make the things that you desire come to fruition. Most people are passive observers and let life float on by. We are the creators of our destiny!

Why does it matter?

We get to choose how we want to live our life, and the choices that we make will bring us what we ask for and believe.

If you keep believing you are poor and have no money, you will always be poor and broke! If you believe that you are stuck in a crappy job, you will still have the same job! And if you want to continue to stay and live in an unhappy relationship, you will!

You see, we get to choose our life and circumstances (I am not talking physical illnesses here) to live our life to the fullest, so we need to choose what we want and then take radical action to make it happen. No one else can do it for us.

How do you do it?

Are you ready to start living your dream life, the life that you desire? Yell out loud "YES I AM!" Awesome!

Go back to Chapter 10 to see the goals that you wrote down. Start to be aware of your thoughts; it's time to create radical action. Aligning your thoughts with your goals will move you in the right direction of achieving them. Begin to act as though you have already reached your goals and you are living the life you want. Don't worry about anything; keep moving forward, and you will begin to reap the rewards.

If you are experiencing any of the following signs and symptoms, then you are on the pathway to discovering your true identity and living your dream:

- A tendency to think and act spontaneously rather than on fears based on past experiences

- An unmistakable ability to enjoy each moment

- A loss of interest in judging other people and judging yourself

- A loss of interest in interpreting the actions of others

- A loss of interest in conflict
- A lack of ability to worry (this is a severe symptom)

- Repeated, overwhelming episodes of appreciation and frequent attacks of smiling

- Frequent feelings of connectedness with others and with nature

- An increasing tendency to let things happen, rather than making them happen

- Increased susceptibility to the love extended by others as well as the uncontrollable urge to spread it.

Notes

SPEND TIME ALONE

What is it?

In today's busy, stressful world, I don't think people take enough time for alone time. For some people, they equate alone time with being lonely, depressed or antisocial. I believe that spending time with yourself is very healthy and has a lot of benefits that go along with it.

Why does it matter?

I am very passionate about helping others, and I love my work. I teach approximately 15 fitness/pilates/yoga classes a week, and I work privately with clients as well. Helping people on their journey to creating and living their best lives through fitness, health and wellness is very gratifying for me. I do get to have alone time for me, but when I'm "on" all the time and don't have any time to recharge, my body begins to show warning signs when I'm starting to burnout.

Even though I experienced the significant burnout in 2012 (read more in Chapter 18), and some fantastic experiences came out of that time in my life, I never want to go there again. In the last five years, I have become very proactive in making time for myself.

Burnout can creep up on us if we're not in control of our lives and can show up as:

- getting tired quicker than normal
- eating the wrong things or losing our appetite
- feeling emotionally exhausted
- feeling mentally drained
- becoming increasingly cranky with our loved ones
- getting sick

There is a vast difference between being lonely and being alone. Being lonely can happen even if you're sitting next to a loved one on the couch! It can show up as a dull ache in your heart, or feelings of sadness that you can't shake off. It's the sensation of abandonment or isolation that you feel in your gut.

It's a feeling that something is missing in your life. We don't choose to be lonely.

How do you do it?

Being alone is a choice that people make. It's a feeling of completeness, not having to depend on another to fill your time, to enjoy your own company, to feeling alive and very present!

Alone time has many benefits, and when I get the chance, I make time for me. Whether it is going for a walk, a bike ride by myself or spending an entire weekend working in my garden and hanging out with Ruby (my kitty), I look forward to these few precious hours. I can feel my body, mind, and spirit recharging.

How do you spend your alone time? Write it here:

_____

_____

_____

There are so many benefits to spending time alone; here are a few reasons to make time for you:

1. You get to learn about yourself; to know who you truly are.

2. Sometimes doing nothing is the best thing you can do to relax, restore, renew and recharge your body, mind, and spirit.

3. It gives you time to focus on your goals, dreams, and desires.

So, what are some ways of spending time alone? Here are a few:

- Take yourself on a date to your favourite restaurant
- Turn off the phone
- Take a day off
- Go for a walk in your favourite park
- Find a peaceful place to meditate
- Play in the garden
- Relax and listen to your favourite music
- Go for a drive and crank the tunes
- Play in the water; go for a swim, kayak, paddleboard, or float down the river

Whatever you decide to do to recharge, enjoy every moment. You are worth it! 💜

Spend time alone in the quiet of your own thoughts and then emerge as the person you really are on the inside, and not the one you think you must pretend to be"
Michelle Sandl

LOVE

What is it?

Love is patient; love is kind. It does not envy; it does not boast, it is not proud. It is not rude, it is not self-seeking, it is not easily angered, and it keeps no records of wrongs. Love does not delight in evil but rejoices with the truth. It always protects, always trusts, always hopes, and always perseveres.

1Corinthians 13:4-7

Human beings are made up of this one beautiful and amazing thing; LOVE. It is who we are; 100% pure love, and it is what makes the world go around. Unfortunately, many people in this world have never experienced love. They may have experienced trauma that has buried the feeling of love deep within them. They have learned to put up walls to protect themselves, so they don't get hurt again. Knowing this makes me very sad because we all deserve to be loved and to love. It's time for us to spread the love. 🖤

"When the power of love overcomes the love of power,
the world will attain peace."
                                    Jimmy Hendrix

I'm sure you will agree that there are many different types of love. The kinds of loves that we give to our family, our friends, our pets, and even our favourite foods are entirely different styles of love than what we have for our partner; our life companion. But still, we use the same word. It is easy to understand that confusion is easily made when we communicate. I can say "I love you" to two different people (and mean it), but I am feeling the love differently.

When I was researching the word "love" I came across a list of seven different words that the ancient Greek used to define "love":

Philia: the love that you have for friends; friendship

Ludus: this is playful love, like childish love, flirting or uncommitted love

Eros: sexual or passionate love. In Greek myth, it is understood that when we are struck from Cupid's arrow, we 'fall' in love

Pragma: long-standing love. This love is the practical love that is usually shared by a long-married couple.

Agape: this is the unconditional love, or universal/divine love that we have for nature, strangers, and god

Storge:(pronounced store-gae) this is natural affection, the love you share with your family

Philautia: the love of the self (negative or positive)

I have experienced all of these different types of love, but I didn't realize that each had a different name; it makes so much sense now.

Why does it matter?

Love is what we need to spread around us, especially nowadays with all the hatredness, fear and struggles that are going on in our world today. I know the world will be a much better place if we can show each other more love.

How do you do it?

We need to learn how to love one another freely, to recognize our self in each other and work together to create unity in the world. We may not be able to change the world, but we can start changing our corners of the world and show others how to change theirs. There are many ways we can show and give love to people we know, as well as to strangers:

- Give a helping hand
- Be friendly; smile and make eye contact
- Make small talk
- Listen to someone without judgement
- Volunteer your time
- Give without expecting to receive something in return
- Be courteous

- Pay it forward by paying for a stranger's items
- Hold the door open for someone
- Donate clothing

Can you think of other ways you can show your love to others?

_____

_____

_____

Have you ever 'been in love' before? You know, the love that gives you butterflies in your tummy and makes you blush when you think of your lover? Or simply smiling because you're happy and life is pretty easy? I'm happy to say that when I've been away from my hubby for a period of time, I still get those butterflies when I see him again, even after 31 years…(sigh)

Love for your partner can also change over time. If we take into consideration the first four different loves listed at the beginning of this chapter (page 122) we can feel all those loves with the same person. When my hubby and I first met, it was through a mutual friend, and we became fast friends (Philia). As the friendship developed, and we were in each other's company more, we began to flirt with each other (Ludus) and, eventually, we were struck with Cupid's arrow and fell in love (Eros). All of this happened within a year and five years later we were married. It hasn't been an easy 31 years, but the love (Pragma) has brought us through and over all the barriers that we have had to face. We have true love for each other and we know that we can face anything...together.

The book *"The Five Love Languages"* by Dr. Gary Chapman, a marriage expert, is a great book and I highly recommend it if you are interested in learning how to truly love your partner. His approach to helping you experience giving love, as well as receiving it, can help your current relationships flourish once you know how the other person experiences feeling loved.

Essentially, according to Dr. Chapman, there are five ways we can be loved, and how we were shown love growing up by our tribe is how we get our 'love tank' filled by another. When you know your partner's love language, it will make all the difference in the world by showing how much you do love him/her with the right love language. There is nothing worse than loving gestures going unacknowledged or feeling like your partner doesn't care.

I first read the book 18 years ago when I was on a much-needed vacation with my hubby. He wasn't interested in reading it but he did fill out the Personal Profile Assessment that was included in the back of the book for me, so I could know how to fill up his love tank. Of course, I filled it out for him too.

THE FIVE LOVE LANGUAGES ARE:

Words of Affirmation: A person feels loved by compliments being given to him/her. Being told that he/she is fantastic, looks great, is so smart, and is loved, are the right ways of filling his/her love tank. On the other end of the spectrum, insults can blow apart this person's tank.

Receiving Gifts: For some people, receiving a gift makes them feel very loved and appreciated. It doesn't mean that the person is materialistic; perhaps it was the way that he/she was shown growing up, being given gifts in replace of hugs and compliments.

Acts of Service: Actions speak louder than words sometimes and doing an act of service for someone is truly appreciated and a person can feel much loved. I remember a friend telling me that whenever she would come home, and the kitchen was clean, she felt loved by her hubby.

Quality Time: This term simply means undivided attention from another. A lot of my friends were married to fishermen when I was living in a northern fishing city and spent many months alone raising their children during fishing season. The one thing they craved when their hubbies came home was spending time with him alone. This language is about giving your total attention to another.

Physical Touch: It's important to point out here that Dr. Chapman is talking about appropriate touch, and not just in the bedroom. If you were hugged a lot as a child, chances are this is one of your love languages. I am a huge advocate for hugging and love to receive hugs too. Other ways of experiencing physical touch that fill the love tank are holding hands, a gentle touch on the shoulder, tickles, hand squeezing or a light kiss.

I'm sure after reading the five love languages, you can see how important it is to know how to fill up your partner's love tank; to make him/her always feel special.

LOVE MAKES THE WORLD GO AROUND

When I was growing up, Mum and Dad always showed love to strangers. I remember many occasions that they opened their hearts to others. On our numerous car trips up to London to visit relatives, they would almost always stop and pick up a person in uniform who was hitchhiking (both Mum and Dad served in the forces) and give them a ride to their destination. When downtown, Dad wouldn't hesitate to cross the street to help a senior who was on the other side of the road and was having a hard time crossing it. They were always taking meals to friends and neighbours who were sick or injured and needed help.

I took my daughters on a trip to Vancouver a couple of years ago. We had just come out from having our dinner when a fellow approached me for money. I asked if he was hungry and then my daughters witnessed me taking him to a nearby local fast food restaurant (his choice) and buying him dinner. Most often, at least once a week, I buy someone lunch. It's usually someone standing outside the local grocery store asking for money. I don't give money, but I will always go in and buy them a great lunch, complete with a drink and a bottle of water.

In our city, a few of the local stores will put up Christmas Trees every December with names attached of children and seniors. I always delight in taking a couple of those names and returning with special gifts that I have purchased for those people.

Just this past year, my daughter and her hubby decided to help a family at Christmas by supplying them with a Christmas feast. They put the word out to their friends and they not only gave one Christmas dinner away, but they also gave out 13 more meals! Each complete with all the fixings; a dinner that would be a delight to anyone. This just goes to show that, together with their friends, they changed their corner of the world.

Notes

CONCLUSION

I hope that the tips in this book will help you on your journey of finding peace, love, happiness and joy, so that you can live life to the fullest.

We are here in this beautiful place we call earth to experience all of those feelings every day.

At the end of each class I teach every day, I leave my participants with the following quote:

"Have a great day unless you choose otherwise."

You see, it is your choice! Are you going to have a great day? Only you can decide whether you will or not. I wish you one from the bottom of my heart. ♥

For resource materials that support the content of this book, please visit www.rhonaparsons.com/21ways

Notes

WHAT PEOPLE ARE SAYING ABOUT RHONA

"Rhona, you are someone very passionate about sharing your expertise with others, that you teach from the heart to help others with your knowledge, and that you truly want to make a difference in their lives. And I have been blessed to learn from you!" ~ Elara

"Rhona is one of the most honest and passionate people I know. She is in the fitness and health industry because she truly cares about the well being of people. Rhona is the person who inspired, helped and pushed me to become a fitness instructor many years ago and to this day, she is someone who I can turn to anytime when I need help or guidance. She is so eager and willing to share anything and everything she knows with her students, clients and other fitness instructors as well - and she knows A LOT! You always gain valuable insight and information from any class or course you take with her. Rhona continues to inspire and guide me along my fitness career path, and I wouldn't be as successful as I am today without her." ~ Karen C

"Always growing and seeking, Rhona is one of the strongest people I know. She is someone who I've always looked up to; a mentor and anyone would be so fortunate to have her in their lives. She is not afraid to reach for her dreams, and is someone who I always learn from" ~ Peggy B

"Rhona is fun, innovating, and because of her passion for fitness, health, and wellness, she brings out the best in us all. Rhona, you are an inspiration". ~ Sylvie S

"An exceptional person who has demonstrated having incredible sensitivity, Rhona is an influential person whom others are eager to listen to and respect. She is a person who can contribute to making other people's dreams come true and an honest person who gives of herself with no expectation in return. Thank you, Rhona!" ~ Rhonda P

ABOUT THE AUTHOR

"Inspiring Real Purpose and Real Change in the World"

www.rhonaparsons.com

As an author, entrepreneur, Life Coach, a student of the Mind, Body & Spirit theory, a National Fitness Presenter and an Internationally recognized Yoga Instructor, Rhona "lights up" guiding and instructing others to live their best life through fitness, health, and wellness.

Rhona is a highly accomplished National Bender Ball and Barre Above Master Trainer and has followed her love and passion for helping others by developing and teaching fitness and yoga programs for over 21 years. She enjoys a successful fitness and wellness career leading dynamic personal and group fitness classes, core-based Yoga Vinyasa classes as well as instructor-training workshops. Many fitness and yoga instructors have been mentored by Rhona throughout BC and Alberta by attending her own creative Continuing Education approved workshops. Currently, she is teaching her signature course, Antaraka Yoga/Pyfusion, to instructors across Canada.

Rhona lived the first fifteen years of her life in a little village in southern England, and in high school, she was very active in track and field, dance and was on the school Netball team. In 1977, much to Rhona's chagrin, she emigrated to Prince Rupert, BC in Canada with her Mum and Dad, sister and older brother. Depressed and very unhappy, Rhona stopped being active. It wasn't until 1987 when Rhona became a single Mum without a car and three young daughters to look after, that she began walking as a mode of transport. This new way of travelling was the beginning of her becoming active once more; she started taking aerobic classes too to take her mind off the stresses in her life; it worked.

Rhona met her (now) hubby Brian in 1987; he was an avid gym goer, so she joined the gym he went to, and he taught her how to lift weights. After a couple of months, Rhona loved the changes she was feeling in her body, but she knew that she had to do a cardio component to keep her heart healthy and to get her body fitter. The thought of being on a treadmill for an hour at a time didn't excite Rhona, so she began going to more Aerobics classes. The more classes Rhona went to, the more she was inspired to learn, and in 1996 at the age of 35, Rhona became a fitness instructor.

In 1997, Rhona went to her first yoga class and fell in love with the discipline, so a year later she embarked on taking a 500-hour yoga course. During this time, she also received her first level of USUI Reiki and began the journey that would eventually feed her passion helping others through fitness, health, and wellness. In 1999 Rhona went back to College to pursue a career in Physiotherapy. After two semesters, and having two teenage daughters at home, Rhona realized that the profession was out of her grasp, so in 2000, Rhona went to Vancouver and took the STOTT Pilates instructor training course. With the help of Brian, in September of that year, she opened her very own Pilates and Yoga studio, BODYWORKS Fitness & Health.

In 2003, Rhona and Brian moved to Vernon, BC where she worked at a variety of clubs and Yoga studios. In 2005, she was hired as part of a management team and with her team opened a national fitness club. In 2010, due to her hubby's ill-health and her own physical and emotional challenges, Rhona left the club. Without considering her own challenges, she went on to open another fitness club with two partners, but in October 2012, Rhona's mental and physical health caught up to her, and she fell head-on into a nervous breakdown. It was during this time that Rhona's spiritual journey became more apparent to her. She realized that her purpose in life was, and is, to inspire people to practice living a happy life to the fullest. She knew that she couldn't help anyone until she had helped herself. It took about two and a half years for Rhona to feel

100% physically and mentally fit and to start focusing on helping others once again.

With enthusiasm and passion for helping others, Rhona's professional goals are to share her extensive knowledge with you, supporting and motivating you along your journey to better health and longevity. Through Life Coaching, she is here to help you build a strong foundation and to balance your body, mind, and spirit that will enhance your wellbeing, and allow you to enjoy life to its fullest.

Locally, Rhona teaches Pilates, Yoga and Group Fitness classes at various studios and is a Personal Fitness Trainer and Educator. She specializes in Functional Training that includes Posture, Core, Balance, Pelvic Floor Fitness, and Strength Training; helping people with balance and instability. As a body, mind and spirit innovator, Rhona leads annual sold-out weekly Yoga Retreats in Mexico where her clients are treated to five-star luxury while they relax, restore, renew and recharge their body, mind, and spirit.

Rhona is a caring, passionate person who loves her work. She is a unique and focused individual and continuously upgrades her skills to be able to teach and help others. Incredible focus and dedication to her beliefs are always evident, and her ability to motivate clients through her vast knowledge is truly inspiring. Full of boundless energy, fun, and a caring, loving individual,

Rhona is a clear, concise and methodical instructor who motivates others to take care of themselves and be kind to each other.

Rhona is a mother of 3 beautiful daughters, NanaRho to 8 incredible grandchildren, and is married to the love of her life, her firefighter hubby, Brian. She lives her truth by balancing her dedication to her career and clients, and her devotion to her family and their wellbeing.

Rhona offers a free 15-minute consultation to everyone who is looking for a new change in his/her life through fitness, health, and wellness. She can be reached by:

Website: www.rhonaparsons.com/book-online
Email: rhona@rhonaparsons.com
Linked In: linkedin.com/in/rhona-parsons-3b534784
Facebook: Rhona Parsons,
　　　　　　The Balance Coach

88406066R00082

Made in the USA
Middletown, DE
09 September 2018